DAD JOKES

the GOOD.
the BAD.
the TERRIBLE.

Jimmy Niro

 source

TABLE
OF CONTENTS

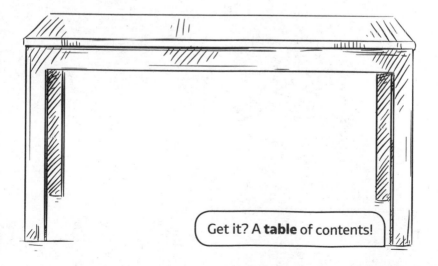

Get it? A **table** of contents!

INTRODUCTION

Q: When does a joke become a **dad** joke?
A: When it becomes ap**parent**!

Ah, the dad joke—humor that reminds us of all the lovable, embarrassing dads out there, both real and fictional. Most joke books try to avoid these jokes—the obvious, the silly, the awkward. But this book steers straight ahead to the absolute cringe-worthy! These are the cheesy puns, overly literal one-liners, and witty quips dads tell that we all know and love (maybe somewhat reluctantly). You'll find jokes on everything from food and animals to professions and traffic, so buckle up, folks! You are about to read some of the best dad jokes imaginable!

ALL ABOUT PEOPLE 'N THINGS

"Dad, will you hand me my **sunglasses**?"

"As soon as you hand me my **dadglasses**, Son."

.... 👨 ....

Q: What did the **pen** say to the other pen?
A: "You're **ink**redible!"

It was easy for me to master **braille** once I got a **feel** for it.

·   〰   ·

Q: What did one **eye** say to the other **eye**?
A: "**Between you and me**, something smells."

·   〰   ·

"Dad, can you put my shoes on?"

"I don't think they'd fit me."

·   〰   ·

I tell **dad** jokes but I have no kids. I'm a faux **pa**.

·   〰   ·

Q: What do you call a small **parent**?
A: A mini**mum**!

I'm terrified of **elevators**. I'm going to start taking **steps** to avoid them.

.... 〰 ....

As a child, it was my dream to make a perfect bar of **soap**, but somehow it just **slipped** away.

.... 〰 ....

Q: What do **snow**men do in their spare time?
A: They just **chill**.

.... 〰 ....

Did you hear about the man who invented the **knock-knock** joke? He won the **No Bell** Prize.

.... 〰 ....

Q: What do you call someone with no **body** and no **nose**?
A: **Nobody knows**.

Do you want to hear a joke about **paper**? Never mind; it's **tear**able.

· ∼ ·

My father and I were in the car traveling to a family outing. On the way, after passing a graveyard, my dad asked, "Did you know that's a popular cemetery?"

"No, why?" I responded.

"People are just dying to get in there!" he replied.

After I groaned, he continued, in all seriousness, "But really, did you know I can't be buried there?"

"Why not, Dad?" I asked, surprised.

"Because I'm not dead yet!"

· ∼ ·

The bank robber took a **bath** after a heist. He wanted to make a **clean** getaway.

· ∼ ·

Q: Why did the boy bring a **ladder** to chorus?
A: He wanted to sing **higher**!

Did you hear about the **houses** that fell in love? It was a **lawn**-distance relationship.

* * *

Q: Why did the belt go to **jail**?
A: Because it **held up** a pair of pants!

* * *

Our wedding was so beautiful, even the **cake** was in **tiers**.

* * *

Never buy anything with **Velcro**®. It's a total **rip-off**.

* * *

Q: Why did the **scarecrow** win an award?
A: Because he was **outstanding** in his field.

Did you hear about the guy who invented **Life Savers**®? They say he made a **mint**.

⸺ 〰 ⸺

"Dad, are you going to **take** a bath?"

"No, I'm **leaving** it where it is."

⸺ 〰 ⸺

Did you hear about the fire in the **shoe** factory? Hundreds of **soles** were lost.

⸺ 〰 ⸺

I **worked out** so hard, the police put me in jail. I was charged with resisting a **rest**.

⸺ 〰 ⸺

Q: Why can't you have a nose that is **twelve inches** long?
A: Because then it would be a **foot**.

Did you hear about the **calendar** thief? He got **twelve months**.

.... ⟨⟩ ....

Q: Can February **march**?
A: No, but April **may**.

.... ⟨⟩ ....

The cops just arrested the **Energizer**® Bunny™!
They charged him with **battery**.

.... ⟨⟩ ....

I got an expensive bill from the **electric** company
this month. I was **shocked**.

.... ⟨⟩ ....

Q: What did one **bell** say to the other?
A: "Be my valen**chime**!"

I gave all my dead **batteries** away today, free of **charge**.

·································· ﹅ ··································

Q: What's black, white, and **read** all over?
A: A **newspaper**.

·································· ﹅ ··································

I used to hate facial **hair**, but then it started **growing** on me.

·································· ﹅ ··································

A group of chess enthusiasts checked into a hotel after a large chess tournament. Rather than going straight to their rooms, the group stayed together in the lobby discussing the day's events and their recent victories.

After an hour, the manager of the hotel entered the lobby and asked them to disperse.

"But why?" they asked.

The manager answered, "Because I can't stand chess nuts boasting in an open foyer."

Did you hear about the **perfume** thief? She was convicted of **fragrancy**.

. . . .

Q: When does a bed grow **longer**?
A: At night, because two **feet** are added to it.

. . . .

My **recliner** and I go way **back**.

. . . .

My wife asked me to stop singing "Wonderwall" to her. **I said maybe**.

. . . .

"Dad, how do I **look**?"

"With your **eyes**."

Somebody stole all my **lamps**. I couldn't be more **delighted**.

.... 🔶 ....

Q: Why are there no **knock-knock** jokes about America?
A: Because freedom **rings**.

.... 🔶 ....

I'd tell you a joke about **beds**, but it hasn't been **made up** yet.

.... 🔶 ....

Q: Who is the **strongest** thief?
A: A shop**lifter**.

.... 🔶 ....

Did you hear about the granny who plugged her electric blanket into the **toaster** by mistake? She spent the night **popping** out of bed.

Q: What kind of **photos** do teeth take?
A: Tooth**pics**!

. . . . 〜 . . . .

The shovel was a **ground**breaking invention.

. . . . 〜 . . . .

My grandfather has the heart of a **lion** and a lifetime ban at the **zoo**.

. . . . 〜 . . . .

Q: How do you make a band**stand**?
A: Take away their **chairs**.

. . . . 〜 . . . .

My ex **misses** me, but her **aim** is improving.

. . . . 〜 . . . .

Q: Why did the man throw the **clock** out the window?
A: Because he heard **time** flies.

If **prisoners** could take their own mugshots, they'd be called **cell**-fies.

.... 〰 ....

"Dad, you put your shoes on the wrong feet!"

"But they're the only feet I have."

.... 〰 ....

Is this **pool** safe for swimming? It **deep** ends.

.... 〰 ....

When I was feeling down, my friend told me, "It could be worse. You could be stuck underground in a **hole full of water**." I knew he meant **well**.

.... 〰 ....

Q: What do you call a boomerang that doesn't come back?
A: A stick.

Bells are really obedient objects. They sound off only when they are **tolled**.

.... 👄 ....

I used to work in a store that required customers to use an account number at checkout. When shoppers were ready, I would ask them for their number, enter it manually, and then ring them up.

One day, a family who I hadn't seen before entered, and the mom and kids wandered off to start shopping. Meanwhile, the dad approached me while I was serving customers, announced his account number to me, and then ran off to join his family without saying anything else. I thought that was weird, but I went on serving.

About ten minutes later, the family stood in line for my register. When it came to the point where I should have asked for their account number, the dad grinned at me, and I realized what was going on. Fortunately, I have an unusually good memory for numbers and, without skipping a beat, I reeled off the account he told me earlier. The children both gasped and their eyes grew wide, looking at their dad in awe.

As I rang up the shopping items, I heard the dad say, "See? I told you they were psychic."

Stairs can't be trusted. They're always **up** to something.

· 🥸 ·

Q: What's **musical** and **handy** in a supermarket?
A: A **Chopin Liszt**.

· 🥸 ·

Yesterday I ate a **clock**. It was very **time** consuming, especially when I went back for **seconds**.

· 🥸 ·

I wanted to wear my **camo** pants today, but I couldn't **find** them.

· 🥸 ·

"Dad, I'm cold."

"Go stand in a **corner**. It's **90 degrees**."

My grandmother put **wheels** on her rocking chair. I guess she wanted to rock and **roll**.

⚬⚬⚬⚬⚬⚬⚬⚬⚬⚬⚬⚬⚬ 〰 ⚬⚬⚬⚬⚬⚬⚬⚬⚬⚬⚬⚬⚬

Q: What's Whitney Houston's favorite type of coordination?
A: HAND EYEEEEEEEE.

⚬⚬⚬⚬⚬⚬⚬⚬⚬⚬⚬⚬⚬ 〰 ⚬⚬⚬⚬⚬⚬⚬⚬⚬⚬⚬⚬⚬

I tried to tell a joke about **Julius Caesar**, but it was all over the place. I guess you could say the joke was **roamin'**.

⚬⚬⚬⚬⚬⚬⚬⚬⚬⚬⚬⚬⚬ 〰 ⚬⚬⚬⚬⚬⚬⚬⚬⚬⚬⚬⚬⚬

Q: Where do **mermaids** go to see movies?
A: The **dive**-in.

⚬⚬⚬⚬⚬⚬⚬⚬⚬⚬⚬⚬⚬ 〰 ⚬⚬⚬⚬⚬⚬⚬⚬⚬⚬⚬⚬⚬

Did you hear about the **musician** who was arrested? She got herself into **treble**.

"I'll call you later."

"Don't call me later. Call me Dad."

·····················

Q: Why does Peter Pan always **fly**?
A: He Never**lands**.

·····················

Never cheat in a **limbo** contest. It's the **lowest** thing you can do.

·····················

Q: Why did the girl bring a **ruler** to bed?
A: She wanted to see **how long** she slept.

·····················

I don't have any red **blood** cells, so my doctors are looking in **vein**.

A friend of mine fell into an **upholstery** machine, but it's okay. He has **recovered**.

·························· 〰 ··························

Q: Why did the child **punch** the bed?
A: Her mother told her to **hit** the hay.

·························· 〰 ··························

I tried to go to a **trampoline** park today, but they told me to **bounce**.

·························· 〰 ··························

Q: Which birds **steal** soap from the bath?
A: Robber ducks!

·························· 〰 ··························

I told my doctor that I always get heart**burn** when I eat birthday cake. He said that I should take the **candles** off first.

"Dad, did you get **a hair**cut?"

"No, I got them **all cut**."

* * *

When I realized I ran out of clean **pants** today, I felt really **depleated**.

* * *

I'd like a new **boomerang**, but I can't seem to be able to **throw** the old one away.

* * *

Q: Why are Saturday and Sunday so **strong**?
A: Because the rest of the days are **weak**days.

* * *

I'm having trouble organizing a **hide-and-seek** league. Good players are **hard to find**.

Q: What is the **range** of a tuba?

A: Twenty yards if you've got a good arm.

- - - - - - - - - - - - - - - - - -

"Dad, are you **all right**?"

"No, I'm half left and half right."

- - - - - - - - - - - - - - - - - -

There's a new type of **broom** out. It's **sweeping** the nation.

- - - - - - - - - - - - - - - - - -

Q: Why can't **glad**iators cry?

A: Because they're never **sad**.

- - - - - - - - - - - - - - - - - -

I think I have bad **posture**, but it's just a **hunch**.

Today at school, a classmate accidentally hit me with the door as he exited a classroom. Instead of saying sorry, he just looked me over and said, "You're pretty cute," and walked away.

At first, I was really offended that he didn't apologize for hurting me, but then I realized I was literally hit on. I guess you could say that he adored me.

.... 👨 ....

My wife gets mad at me for hiding kitchen **utensils**. But that's a **whisk** I'm willing to take.

.... 👨 ....

Q: How can you **shorten** a bed?
A: Don't sleep **long** in it.

.... 👨 ....

Most **chairs** are **sat**in.

Did you hear about the **printers** that learned to play musical instruments? Their band started to **paper jam**.

.... 〰 ....

Q: What do you get if you have **strep throat** on Friday?
A: Saturday Night **Fever**.

.... 〰 ....

I was **wondering** why the baseball was getting bigger. Then it **hit** me.

.... 〰 ....

Q: What do you call the fear of being trapped in a **chimney**?
A: **Claus**trophobia.

.... 〰 ....

I **hung up** a copy of the U.S. constitution on my wall. I call it the **decoration** of independence.

Q: How do you fix a **broken** tuba?
A: With a tuba **glue**.

····························· ~ ·····························

Did you hear about the man who misspelled a
name on a **headstone**? He made a **grave** mistake.

····························· ~ ·····························

"Dad, your jokes are so bad
it's like punishment."

"You mean **PUN**ishment?"

DANGEROUS DINOS & MONSTERS

Q: What are prehistoric creatures called when they **sleep**?
A: **Dinosnores**!

Q: What did the mother **ghost** say to the baby ghost?
A: "**Spook** when you're spooken to."

Q: How do you communicate with the **Loch Ness** Monster?
A: Drop her a **line**.

Q: What is a **ghost**-proof bicycle?
A: One with no **spooks** in it.

. . . .   〰   . . . .

Did you hear about the monster with **five** legs? His trousers fit him like a **glove**.

. . . .   〰   . . . .

Q: What **followed** the dinosaur?
A: Its **tail**!

. . . .   〰   . . . .

Q: When do **ghosts** play tricks on each other?
A: On April **Ghouls'** Day.

. . . .   〰   . . . .

Q: What do **sea monsters** eat for dinner?
A: **Fish** and **ships**.

A visitor at the natural history museum asked a museum employee, "Excuse me, can you tell me how old the skeleton of that *Tyrannosaurus Rex* is?"

The employee replied, "It is precisely sixty million and three years, two months, and eighteen days old."

The visitor was astounded and said, "How can you know that number with such precision?"

"Well, when I started working here," the employee responded, "one of the scientists told me that the skeleton was sixty million years old—and that was precisely three years, two months, and eighteen days ago."

.... 👨 ....

Q: How do you stop a monster from **digging** up your garden?
A: Take his **shovel** away.

.... 👨 ....

Q: What's a **monster's** favorite play?
A: *Romeo and **Ghoul**iet.*

Q: What **monster** flies his kite in a rainstorm?
A: Benjamin **Frankenstein**.

A sore **mummy** needs a **Cairo**practor.

Q: What's the most **evil** chord?
A: D min.

Q: What is a **ghost's** favorite fruit?
A: **Boo**nana!

Q: What kind of monster is safe to put in the washing machine?
A: A wash and **wear wolf**.

Q: Why did the **haunted** house dislike storms?

A: Because the rain dampened its **spirits**.

Q: Why did the **monster** see a psychiatrist?

A: He felt **abominable**.

Did you hear about the **ghost** comedian? He was **boo**ed off stage.

Q: What do you call a **clever** monster?

A: Frank**einstein**.

Q: Why are **ghosts** such bad liars?

A: Because you can see right **through** them.

A ghost was barred from entry to a local **pub**. They don't serve **spirits**.

.... 🥸 ....

Q: Why don't **skeletons** ever go trick or treating?
A: Because they have **no body** to go with.

.... 🥸 ....

Q: How did the monster cure his **sore throat**?
A: He spent all day **gargoyl**ing.

.... 🥸 ....

If you forget to pay for your **exorcism**, will you be re**possessed**?

.... 🥸 ....

Q: Where do baby **ghosts** go during the day?
A: Day **scare** centers.

Q: What kind of street does a **ghost** like best?
A: A **dead** end.

. . . . 〜 . . . .

Dr. Frankenstein had been working all day and night in his laboratory. Once he finally took a break, he asked his assistant, Igor, "Have you seen my latest invention, Igor? It's a new pill consisting of 50 percent glue and 50 percent aspirin."

Puzzled, Igor inquired, "But what is it for, doctor?"

Dr. Frankenstein answered, "For monsters with splitting headaches, of course."

. . . . 〜 . . . .

Q: What do you get if you cross a tall green monster with a **fountain pen**?
A: The **Ink**redible Hulk.

. . . . 〜 . . . .

Q: What do you get when dinosaurs **crash** their cars?
A: Tyrannosaurus **wrecks**!

Q: What do you get when you cross a snowman with a vampire?
A: Frostbite.

. . . . 〰 . . . .

Q: What did the **monster** say when he saw a rush hour train full of passengers?
A: "Oh good! A **chew-chew** train!"

. . . . 〰 . . . .

Q: What would you get if you crossed a dinosaur with a **pig**?
A: Jurassic **pork**!

. . . . 〰 . . . .

Q: What did one **invisible** man say to the other?
A: "Long time **no see**."

. . . . 〰 . . . .

Dr. Frankenstein went to a **bodybuilding** competition. It was a terrible misunderstanding.

Q: What's the first thing the **taxi** driver said to the wolf?
A: Where, wolf?

.... 〰 ....

Q: What is a **monster's** favorite drink?
A: Demonade.

.... 〰 ....

Q: What do you get when you cross Bambi with a **ghost**?
A: Bam**boo**.

ENGLISH IS EASY

AS ABC

I bought the **thesaurus** I've always wanted, but when I opened it, all the pages were blank. I have **no words** to describe how angry I am.

Q: Why did Stalin only write in **lowercase**?
A: Because he hated **capitalism**.

Q: Where can you learn how to make the best **ice cream**?
A: **Sundae** school.

To the person who stole my copy of **Microsoft Office**: I will find you. You have my **Word**.

.... 👨 ....

Q: What is **smarter** than a talking cat?
A: A **spelling** bee!

.... 👨 ....

Q: Where do **typists** go to get a drink?
A: The **Space Bar**.

.... 👨 ....

You can't run through a **campsite**. You can only ran, because it's past **tents**.

.... 👨 ....

Q: Why do bees **hum**?
A: Because they don't know the **words**.

.... 👨 ....

Don't spell "**part**" backwards. It's a **trap**!

Q: What's another name for **Santa's** elves?
A: Subordinate **Claus**es.

· ·

A small local newspaper announced it was having a pun contest. A middle-aged man who loved jokes decided to enter. After narrowing down a list of his favorites, he sent ten different puns in the hopes that at least one would win. Unfortunately, no pun in ten did.

· ·

Q: What's the **longest** word in the English language?
A: "S**mile**s," because there is a mile between the first and last letters.

· ·

I visited a school recently and was amazed by the **dry-erase** boards. They're re**mark**able.

Q: How does a pig **write** home?
A: With a pig**pen**.

Q: Why wasn't the **geometry** teacher at school?
A: Because she sprained her **angle**!

I ordered a book about **puns** last week, but I **didn't get it**.

Q: What's a **hamburger's** favorite story to read?
A: Hansel and **Gristle**!

Q: What does an **educated owl** say?
A: **Whom**.

Libraries are just too strict. They always go by the **books**.

.... 〰 ....

Q: How do **billboards** communicate?
A: **Sign** language.

.... 〰 ....

Q: What kind of **book** did Frankenstein's monster like to read?
A: One with a cemetery **plot**.

.... 〰 ....

Did you hear about the **English** professor who went to jail? She got a full **sentence**.

.... 〰 ....

Q: What's the worst thing about **ancient history** class?
A: The teacher tends to **Babylon**.

I was accused of being a **plagiarist**. **Their words**, not mine.

······································· 〰 ·······································

Q: What's the difference between **ignorance** and **indifference**?
A: I don't know and **I don't care**!

······································· 〰 ·······································

An Englishman, a Frenchman, a Spaniard, and a German were out for a walk when they stopped to watch a street performer who was excellent at juggling.

The juggler noticed that the four men had a bad view from where they stood in the crowd, so he climbed on a large wooden box and shouted, "Can you all see me now?"

"Yes."

"Oui."

"Sí."

"Ja."

······································· 〰 ·······································

Q: How far do **burgers** go in school?
A: Through **cow**llege.

I just learned **sign** language. It's pretty **handy**.

.... 〰 ....

Q: Where did the **piglets** study their ABCs?
A: At a school for higher **loining**.

.... 〰 ....

I was really upset after my friend broke my favorite **pen**. He said, "Don't worry, I'll make this **write**!"

.... 〰 ....

Q: Why are fish so **smart**?
A: They are always in **schools**!

.... 〰 ....

Q: What is a **pirate's** favorite letter?
A: You would think "**R**," but it's actually the "**C**."

I was carrying a **nine-foot book** the other day and a woman asked me what I was doing. I said, "Oh, it's a **long story**."

* * *

Q: What subject in school do **cattle** like the most?
A: **Cow**culus.

* * *

Did you hear about the **cross-eyed** teacher? He couldn't control his **pupils**!

* * *

Q: What did the pencil say to the paper?
A: "I **dot** my **eyes** on you."

* * *

My mom bought me a cheap **dictionary** for my birthday. I couldn't find the **words** to thank her.

Q: What does a **thesaurus** eat for breakfast?
A: A **synonym** roll.

I have a master's degree in being **ignored**. No one seems to **care**.

Q: What shoes do **linguists** wear?
A: **Converse**.

FOOD FOR THOUGHT

"Dad, will you **make me** a sandwich?"

"**Poof!** You're a sandwich!"

⸰⸰⸰⸰⸰⸰⸰⸰⸰⸰⸰⸰⸰⸰⸰⸰⸰⸰⸰⸰⸰⸰ ➳ ⸰⸰⸰⸰⸰⸰⸰⸰⸰⸰⸰⸰⸰⸰⸰⸰⸰⸰⸰⸰⸰

My son just threw a **milk** carton at me. How **dairy**?

⸰⸰⸰⸰⸰⸰⸰⸰⸰⸰⸰⸰⸰⸰⸰⸰⸰⸰⸰⸰⸰⸰ ➳ ⸰⸰⸰⸰⸰⸰⸰⸰⸰⸰⸰⸰⸰⸰⸰⸰⸰⸰⸰⸰⸰

Q: Why was the **burger** thrown out of the army?
A: He couldn't pass **mustard**.

Q: Why do hamburgers make good **baseball** players?
A: They're great at the **plate**!

. . . .

Q: How do you make an apple **puff**?
A: **Chase** it around the garden.

. . . .

I was going to tell you a **pizza** joke, but it's way too **cheesy**.

. . . .

Q: How did the **hipster** burn his tongue?
A: He drank his coffee before it was **cool**.

. . . .

Q: What do you call a cat who eats **lemons**?
A: A **sour**puss!

There was a baker's assistant named Richard the Pourer, and his job was to pour the dough mixture that the baker needs while making sausage rolls. One day, Richard noticed he was running low on one of the necessary spices for the rolls, so he sent a young worker from the bakery to go buy more at the store.

Upon arriving at the shop, the young man was asked if he needed help finding anything, but he realized he had forgotten the name of the ingredient. All he could do was tell the shopkeeper that he needed a spice for Richard the Pourer, for batter for wurst.

.... 👨 ,,

Q: Why did the **banana** go to the doctor?
A: It wasn't **peel**ing well.

.... 👨 ....

Q: What do you call a **fake** noodle?
A: An **impasta**.

.... 👨 ....

My **friend** and I like to try new food together.
We're taste **buds**.

Q: What do you call an **average** potato?
A: A **common**tater.

. . . .   ⌣   . . . .

Q: What did the **baby** corn say to the **mama** corn?
A: "Where's **pop**corn?"

. . . .   ⌣   . . . .

Did you hear about the **cheese** factory that
exploded in France? There was nothing left but
de **Brie**.

. . . .   ⌣   . . . .

Q: How can you make a basset hound **fast**?
A: Take away its **food**!

. . . .   ⌣   . . . .

Q: Why did the **coffee** file a police report?
A: It got **mug**ged.

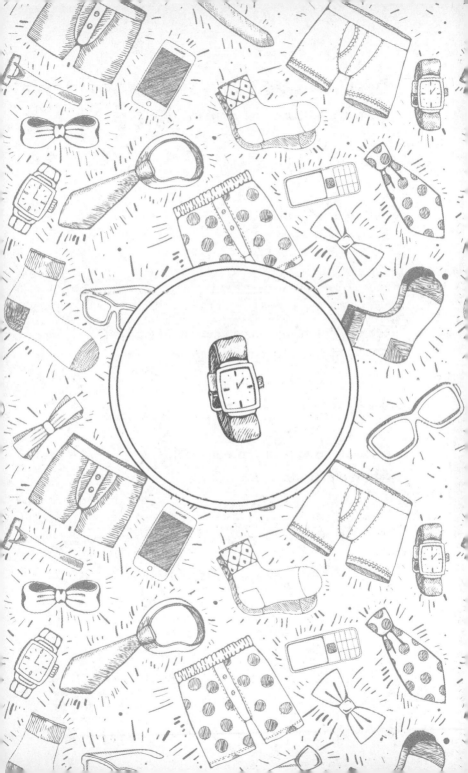

Q: What did the cocktail say to the **swizzle stick**?

A: "You **stir** something inside me."

· 〰 ·

I **threw** butter out the window because I wanted to see a butter**fly**.

· 〰 ·

Q: Why did the banana go out with the **prune**?

A: Because he couldn't find a **date**.

· 〰 ·

Q: What do you call a cow on the **floor**?

A: **Ground** beef.

· 〰 ·

This may come across as **cheesy**, but I think you're **grate**.

Q: What is your **dog's** favorite breakfast?
A: Pooched eggs!

Did you hear the **song** about the tortilla? Actually, it was more of a **wrap**.

Q: What do you use to determine if a **burger** is hot enough?
A: A thermo**meat**er!

"Dad, will you **fix** dinner?"

"I didn't know it was **broken**!"

Q: What is red and sometimes **explodes** in the fruit section?
A: A pome**grenade**.

Did anybody go to the **donut** party? I heard it was **jam**-packed.

.... ~ ....

Q: What did the **grape** do when it was stepped on?
A: It let out a little **wine**.

.... ~ ....

Q: What does **Batman**™ like in his drinks?
A: Just ice.

.... ~ ....

I knew I shouldn't have had the **seafood**. I'm feeling a little **eel**.

.... ~ ....

Q: What do you yell at a **cheese** thief?
A: "That's **na'cho** cheese!"

Q: Why do hamburgers make poor **witnesses**?
A: They won't talk no matter how you **grill** them!

· ·

Did you hear about the **donut** maker retiring? He was fed up with the **hole** business.

· ·

Q: Where do birds meet for coffee?
A: In a nest-café!

· ·

Q: What's the best day to eat **bacon**?
A: **Fry**day.

· ·

Did you know that hamburgers can **hula**? Just order it with a **shake**!

Q: What vegetable needs a **plumber**?

A: A **leek**.

Early one morning, a husband and wife were making breakfast together. The man was making an omelet and beating the eggs with a fork.

The woman said to her husband, "Don't forget to add salt to the eggs, dear."

The man replied, "But I'm already assaulting the egg!"

Q: What **pastry** wanted to rule the world?

A: Attila the **Bun**.

"Dad, your glass of juice is empty. Do you want **another one**?"

"Why would I want **two** empty glasses?"

Q: Why did the **cookie** go to the doctor?
A: It was feeling **crumb-y**!

.... 〰 ....

Q: What happens when two **burgers** fall in love?
A: They live together in holy **meat**rimony!

.... 〰 ....

I used to be a member of the secret **cooking** society, but they kicked me out for spilling the **beans**.

.... 〰 ....

Q: What did one plate say to the other **plate**?
A: "Lunch is **on** me!"

.... 〰 ....

Q: What do **chickens** serve at birthday parties?
A: **Coop**cakes!

You're a **vegetarian**? I think that's a big missed **steak**.

· ～ ·

I have the easiest recipe to make a banana **split**. You just cut it in **half**.

· ～ ·

Q: Why do **hamburgers** love young people?
A: They're **pro-teen**!

· ～ ·

Q: What happens when you drop a hand **gren-egg**?
A: It **egg-splodes**!

· ～ ·

I try to be **cheesy** when I make jokes, but everyone I know is **laughtose** intolerant.

Q: What would you call two **banana** skins?

A: A pair of **slippers**.

.... 〰 ....

Q: What is the **left** side of an apple?

A: The part that you **don't eat**.

.... 〰 ....

Burgers always **laugh** when they are around pickles. They're probably **picklish**.

.... 〰 ....

Q: How do you make a rabbit **stew**?

A: Keep it waiting.

.... 〰 ....

"Dad, what rhymes with 'orange'?"

"No it doesn't."

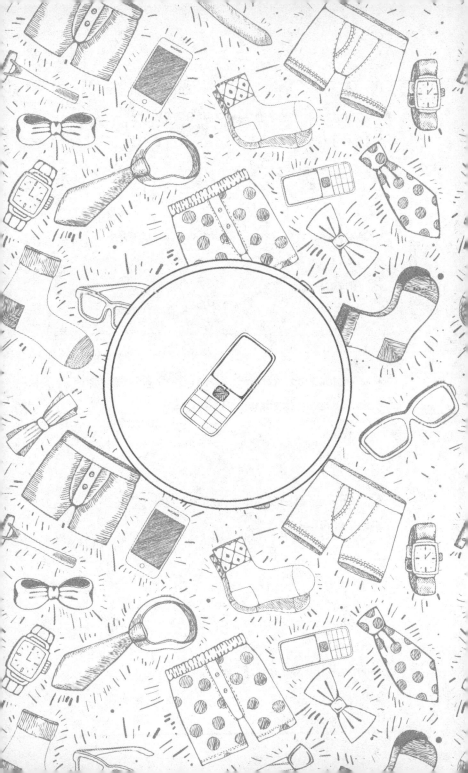

Q: What do you get when you wake up in the morning and realize you're out of **coffee**?
A: A **depresso**.

· ⌣ ·

Q: What do they serve at birthday parties in **heaven**?
A: **Angel** food cake.

· ⌣ ·

Two melons wanted to run away and get **married**, but they realized they cant**aloupe**.

· ⌣ ·

Q: What do **clams** do on their birthdays?
A: **Shell**ebrate!

· ⌣ ·

Q: What can a **whole** apple do that half an apple can't do?
A: It can look **round**.

Time flies like an arrow, but **fruit flies** like a **banana**.

•   👨   •

Q: How do you fix a **broken** pumpkin?
A: With a pumpkin **patch**!

•   👨   •

A woman drove to her local grocery store to go shopping in preparation for Thanksgiving dinner. After collecting the produce and other ingredients she would need, she started picking through the frozen turkeys at the store. Despite the large selection, she couldn't find a turkey big enough for the entire family.

She found a stock boy and asked him, "Excuse me, do these turkeys get any bigger?"

The stock boy replied, "No, ma'am. They're dead."

•   👨   •

Q: Why do sea**gulls** fly over the sea?
A: Because if they flew over the **bay**, they'd be **bagels**.

Did you know hamburgers feel sad at **barbecues**?
They have to meet their old **flames**!

· ·

Q: What do you call an espresso with a **cold**?
A: **Cough**ee.

· ·

When I'm sad, I like to make **pork roast**. That way,
I have a **shoulder** to cry on.

· ·

Q: What is a **cheese** that's made backward?
A: **Edam**.

· ·

Q: What's a **cucumber's** favorite instrument?
A: A **pickle**-o.

The best jokes about **oranges** have a **tang** of truth in them.

.... 〰 ....

Q: Why was the **vegetable** lonely?
A: It had no **pear**.

.... 〰 ....

Q: What did the **pumpkin** say when it was surprised?
A: "Oh my **gourd**ness!"

.... 〰 ....

I stepped on some **cornflakes** this morning. I guess I'm a **cereal** killer.

.... 〰 ....

Q: What is the difference between a banana and a **bell**?
A: You can only **peal** the banana once.

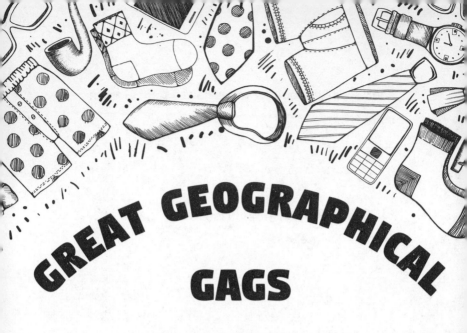

GREAT GEOGRAPHICAL GAGS

Q: What country do **cows** love to visit?
A: Moo Zealand!

.... 👑 ....

Q: In what country is it obvious that you **left**?
A: Uganda.

.... 👑 ....

Ireland's capital is the fastest **growing** city. Every year it's **Dublin**.

Q: What is the biggest **pencil** in the world?
A: **Pennsyl**vania.

.... 🥸 ....

Q: What did **Delaware**?
A: Her **New Jersey**.

.... 🥸 ....

"Dad, how do you feel about going on a **holiday** cruise?"

"Great, we can start at **Christmas** Island and go to **Easter** Island."

.... 🥸 ....

I've heard **Prague** is cool. You should **Czech** it out.

.... 🥸 ....

Q: Why does the Statue of Liberty **stand** in New York Harbor?
A: Because she can't **sit** down!

Q: Where do **hamsters** come from?
A: **Ham**sterdam.

Q: What do you call the place where **parrots** make films?
A: **Polly**wood!

Sweden doesn't export its **cattle** because it wants to keep its **Stockholm**.

Q: What **birds** are found in Portugal?
A: Portu**geese**!

Q: In what **city** will you find the most cows?
A: **Moo York**!

I went to a travel agency last week to get some help planning my next vacation. I had been speaking to an agent for a while about what I would like to do on my trip, but there are so many great destinations in the world that I was having trouble deciding which place I wanted to visit.

"Well, that's easy," the agent told me. "You want to spend some time outdoors, and it would be beautiful in Oslo this time of year. Why don't you think about going there?"

I replied, "Oh no. I have heard Oslo is a particularly dangerous city. There's Norway I'd ever go."

· ~ ·

Q: What is the biggest **pan** in the world?
A: Ja**pan**.

· ~ ·

Q: Which is **smarter**, longitude or latitude?
A: Longitude, because it has 360 **degrees**.

· ~ ·

Florida is a really easy place to **move** to because it has a lot of **keys**.

Q: Where do **burgers** go on vacation?

A: The **Swiss** Alps or the **Cheese**apeake Valley!

.... 👃 ....

Q: What state does the most **laundry**?

A: **Wash**ington.

.... 👃 ....

Q: What kind of **cows** do you find in Alaska?

A: Eski**moos**!

.... 👃 ....

You never see **penguins** in Great Britain because they're afraid of **Wales**.

.... 👃 ....

Q: What did Tennes**see**?

A: The same thing Arkan**sas**.

Q: What's a teacher's favorite nation?
A: Expla**nation**.

.... 🥸 ....

My friends and I could not agree on a vacation together this year, so we decided to take solo trips to different parts of the world.

I didn't expect my roommate would like Cuba, but it turns out she's Havana great time.

Another friend of mine liked Stockholm but was having trouble sleeping, so I wished him Swede dreams.

My third friend decided to tour Croatia. He said the sights were beautiful, but his hotel was Hvar from satisfactory.

And I think I've fallen in love with a girl in South Korea. She may be my Seoul mate.

.... 🥸 ....

Q: What city **cheats** during exams?
A: **Peking**.

Q: What is the best part about living in Switzerland?

A: I'm not sure, but the **flag** is a **big plus**.

· 〜 ·

You could say **German** cities with a lot of people are **kraut**ed.

· 〜 ·

Q: Why did **Eve** want to move to New York?

A: She fell for the Big **Apple**!

· 〜 ·

Q: How was **Rome** split in two?

A: With a pair of **Caesars**!

JUST ANIMALS & BEARLY FUNNY HUMOR

Q: What always goes to bed with **shoes** on?
A: A **horse**!

Q: Why do bears have **hairy** coats?
A: **Fur** protection.

"Dad, can you put the cat **out**?"

"I didn't know the cat was on **fire**!"

Q: What do you call a **boring** dog?
A: A **dull**mation!

Never play games in the **jungle**. There are too many **cheetahs**.

Q: How do you catch a **unique** bird?
A: **Unique** up on it.

Q: Why did the octopus **blush**?
A: It just saw the **bottom** of the ocean.

Q: How can you tell if a snake is a **baby** snake?
A: It has a **rattle**.

A man was admitted into the hospital because he swallowed eight plastic **horses**. His condition is now **stable**.

.... 〰 ....

Q: How does a **bird** with a broken wing manage to land safely?
A: With its **sparrow**chute!

.... 〰 ....

Q: Out of all the animals, what one is the least **interesting**?
A: A **boar**.

.... 〰 ....

Q: To what dog do other dogs tell their **problems**?
A: A **complaint** Bernard!

.... 〰 ....

If you make a **cow** angry, she'll **cream** you.

Q: What did the **orca** say to his valentine?

A: "**Whale** you be mine?"

A man was driving and saw a truck stalled on the side of the highway that had ten penguins standing next to it. The man pulled over and asked the truck driver if he needed any help.

The truck driver replied, "If you can take these penguins to the zoo while I wait for a tow truck that would be great!"

The man agreed and loaded the penguins into the back of his car. Two hours later, the trucker was back on the road and decided to check on the penguins. He went to the zoo, but the penguins weren't there! He returned to his truck and drove around the town, looking for any sign of the penguins, the man, or his car. While driving past a movie theater, the truck driver spotted the guy walking out with the ten penguins.

The truck driver yelled, "What are you doing? You were supposed to take them to the zoo!"

The man replied, "I did, and then I had some extra money so I took them to go see a movie."

Q: What's the best way to **catch** a fish?

A: Have someone **throw** it to you.

.... 👨 ....

Q: Why does a flamingo lift up one leg?

A: Because if it lifted up both legs it would fall over.

.... 👨 ....

I used to search for **shellfish** at the beach until one day when I pulled a **mussel**.

.... 👨 ....

Q: What do you call a cow that fell in a **hole**?

A: A **hole**y cow!

.... 👨 ....

Q: What do you call a crate of **ducks**?

A: A box of **quackers**!

Q: Why have you never seen elephants hiding in trees?

A: Because they're really good at it.

· ~ ·

The **sword**fish is the best-dressed fish. It always looks **sharp**!

· ~ ·

A cowboy had been feeling lonely, so he asked one of his good friends what he could do to make himself feel better. After hearing some advice, the cowboy went to an animal shelter and asked for a dachshund.

One of the volunteers at the animal shelter responded, "Sure, we have some sweet dachshunds here. But if you don't mind my asking, why do you want that breed instead of any other kind of dog?"

The cowboy responded, "My friend suggested I get a long, little doggy."

· ~ ·

Q: Why did the **cow** jump over the moon?

A: To get to the **Milk**y Way!

Q: Why do dogs run in circles?

A: Because it's hard to run in squares!

· ✺ ·

Q: What do you call a cat with **eight** legs that likes to swim?

A: An **octopuss**!

· ✺ ·

Did you see the **horse** that could balance a corncob on its head? It was some **unique corn**.

· ✺ ·

Q: What is a **pig's** favorite Shakespeare play?

A: *Ham*let.

· ✺ ·

Q: Why did the dog jump into the **sea**?

A: He wanted to chase the cat**fish**!

Q: What's the worst kind of **cat** to have?
A: A **cat**astrophe!

.... 〰 ....

Q: Why do kangaroos love **koalas**?
A: Because they have many fine **koalaties**!

.... 〰 ....

I just watched a program about **beavers**. It was the best **dam** program I've ever seen.

.... 〰 ....

Q: What do you call it when one **bull** spies on another bull?
A: A **steak**-out!

.... 〰 ....

Q: What is a **cat's** favorite TV show?
A: The evening **mews**!

Q: What is an **owl's** favorite TV show?
A: *Doctor **Who**.*

.... 〰 ....

Q: Why couldn't the **rabbit** fly home for Easter?
A: He didn't have the **hare** fare.

.... 〰 ....

Did you hear about **Moby Dick's** birthday? He had a **whale** of a party!

.... 〰 ....

Q: What do **cat** actors say on stage?
A: **Tabby** or not tabby!

.... 〰 ....

Q: How many hairs are **in** a dog's tail?
A: None. They are all on the **outside**.

Q: How do you **tune** a fish?
A: With its **scales**!

························· 👨 ·····························

Q: What do you call a crafty **pig**?
A: Cunning**ham**.

························· 👨 ·····························

You know, having **horses** is a real night**mare**.

························· 👨 ·····························

Q: What do you call a **cat** who has joined the Red Cross?
A: A first-aid **kit**!

························· 👨 ·····························

Q: What dog loves to take **bubble** baths?
A: A **shampoo**dle!

Q: What do you get if you cross a **duck** with a firework?
A: A fire**quacker**!

Q: Why did the rabbits go on **strike**?
A: They wanted a better **celery**!

Q: What do **cats** read in the morning?
A: **Mew**spapers!

I've never hunted **bear**, but I have been fishing in **shorts**.

Q: Why did the Clydesdale give the **pony** a glass of water?
A: Because he was a little **horse**!

Q: What do you give a sick **bird**?

A: **Tweet**ment!

Q: What part of a fish **weighs** the most?

A: Its **scales**!

Q: What do you call it when a cat **stops**?

A: A **paws**!

Q: Why do cows like being told **jokes**?

A: Because they like being **amoosed**!

Q: What do you call an **underwater** social network?

A: **Fish**book!

My son wants to dress up as **pest** control for Halloween. I told him to **gopher** it.

· ～ ·

Q: What kind of fish will help you **hear** better?
A: A **herring** aid!

· ～ ·

Q: What do you get when you cross a Doberman with a **bird**?
A: A Doberman **fincher**!

· ～ ·

Q: Why do cats eat **fur balls**?
A: Because they love a good **gag**.

· ～ ·

I hate **insect** puns. They **bug** the heck out of me.

Q: Why did the **rooster** run away?
A: He was **chicken**!

.... 🥸 ....

Q: What do you get if you cross a **cat** with a parrot?
A: A **carrot**!

.... 🥸 ....

Q: Why was the mother **flea** feeling down in the dumps?
A: Because she thought her children were all going to the **dogs**.

.... 🥸 ....

When they told me to stop impersonating a **flamingo**, I put my **foot down**.

.... 🥸 ....

Q: What happened when the cat ate a ball of **wool**?
A: She had **mittens**!

Q: What do you call it when a bunch of **chickens** play hide-and-seek?
A: Fowl play!

.... 〰 ....

A woman brought her Saint Bernard to the vet. She said to the veterinarian, "I'm concerned that my dog is cross-eyed. Is there anything you can do for him, Doctor? Will he be okay?"

"Well, I'm not sure," said the vet. "Let's have a look at him."

The vet picked up the dog and examined his eyes. Finally, she said, "I'm going to have to put him down."

Stunned, the woman exclaimed, "What? Why would you do that? Just because he's cross-eyed?"

The vet replied, "No, because he's really heavy."

.... 〰 ....

Q: What did the judge say when a **skunk** entered the courtroom?
A: Odor in the court!

Q: Why is it easy for **chicks** to talk?
A: Because talk is **cheep**!

Q: What is a **mouse's** favorite game?
A: Hide-and-**squeak**!

An owl lost its **voice**, but it didn't give a **hoot**.

Q: What is the difference between a fish and a **piano**?
A: You can't **tuna** fish.

Q: Why didn't the dog speak to his **foot**?
A: Because it's not polite to talk back to your **paw**!

Q: Why did the **chick** disappoint his mother?
A: He wasn't what he was **cracked** up to be!

. . . .

We can't take our **dog** to the pond anymore because the ducks keep attacking him. I guess that's what we get for having a **pure bread**.

. . . .

Q: What are **cows'** favorite party games?
A: **Moo**sical chairs!

. . . .

Q: What is the definition of **rob**in?
A: A bird who **steals**!

. . . .

Q: What cat **purrs** more than any other?
A: A **Purr**sian!

People can say that **zebras** are carnivores, but they'd be **lion**.

.... 👨 ....

Q: What's the different between a hippo and a **Zippo**®?
A: One is really heavy and the other is a **little lighter**.

.... 👨 ....

Q: What did the seal with a broken arm say to the shark?
A: "Do not consume if seal is broken."

.... 👨 ....

Q: Why can't dogs get **MRIs**?
A: Because only **CAT scan**!

MONEY TALKS

(AND TELLS TERRIBLE JOKES)

A skunk was arrested for **counterfeiting**.
Apparently, he gave out bad **scents**.

Q: How can you **double** your money?
A: By folding it in **half**.

Q: What would you do if a **bull** charged you?
A: Pay whatever it **charged**!

I wasn't surprised when the price of **balloons** went up. There's always **inflation** in that business.

••••••••••••••••••••••••••••••• ⌣ •••••••••••••••••••••••••••••••

Q: Which American president was the least **guilty**?
A: Abraham Lincoln. He was **in a cent**.

••••••••••••••••••••••••••••••• ⌣ •••••••••••••••••••••••••••••••

Q: Why couldn't the **art** dealer pay his rent?
A: He ran out of **Monet**.

••••••••••••••••••••••••••••••• ⌣ •••••••••••••••••••••••••••••••

I spent all my money on seventeenth-century paintings and classical instruments. Now I'm **Baroque**.

••••••••••••••••••••••••••••••• ⌣ •••••••••••••••••••••••••••••••

Q: Why did the **lumberjack** go to the bank?
A: He wanted to open a **shavings** account.

Q: Why was the robber so **secure**?
A: He was a **safe** robber.

· 〜 ·

You can't keep secrets in a **bank**. There are too many **tellers**.

· 〜 ·

I was reading the daily newspaper this morning when I saw a shocking story. About one week ago, the paper had published a report about election fraud. In retaliation for the scandalous exposure, some of the members from the political party that had falsely won attacked the newspaper's offices last night.

I exclaimed to my coworker, "Can you believe they did that?"

"How horrible! What did they do?" She responded.

"Toppled file cabinets, destroyed some papers, smashed computers..."

"Was there any loss of life?"

"No," I said. "It looks like just a monitor-y loss."

Q: Where do Eskimos keep their **money**?
A: In snow**banks**.

Q: Why did the farmer feed **money** to his cow?
A: He wanted **rich** milk!

I kept putting money into the **change** machine yesterday, but nothing **changed**.

Q: Where do **plants** invest their money?
A: In the **stalk** market!

Q: How does the Vatican **pay** bills?
A: They use **Papal**.

Q: What does Santa call his wife at **tax** time?
A: A dependent **Claus**.

.... 〰 ....

Q: When does a female **deer** need money?
A: When she doesn't have a **buck**.

.... 〰 ....

Did you hear that the authorities found all that counterfeited **German** currency? They were question **marks**.

.... 〰 ....

Q: What do you get if you cross a **sorceress** with a millionaire?
A: A very **witch** person.

.... 〰 ....

Q: Where does a **fish** keep its money?
A: In the river**bank**!

A man heard about the discovery of gold in California. Like others hoping to cash in on the big rush, he immediately quit his job, packed his possessions, and headed out west. However, after a year trying to mine for gold, the man gave up and returned to his old home completely penniless. It did not pan out.

.... 〰 ....

Q: How can you get **rich** by eating?
A: Eat **fortune** cookies.

.... 〰 ....

Q: Who makes a **million dollars** a day?
A: Someone who works in a **mint**.

.... 〰 ....

I **flipped a coin** over an issue the other day, but it was a **toss**-up.

Q: Why can't the **bank** manager ride a bike anymore?
A: He lost his **balance**.

.... 🥸 ....

Q: If you went to a concert for **45 cents**, who would play?
A: **50 Cent** and **Nickelback**.

.... 🥸 ....

Q: Why is money called **dough**?
A: Because we all **knead** it.

.... 🥸 ....

Q: When a **duck** goes shopping, does it pay cash or check?
A: Neither. They put it on the **bill**.

.... 🥸 ....

A persistent **banker** wouldn't stop hitting on me, so I asked him to leave me **a loan**.

Q: How else can you **double** your money?
A: Look at it in a **mirror**.

· ▰ ·

A businessman called the passport agency because he had a question about the documents he would need to fly to China for work. After a long discussion about renewing his passport, the clerk reminded him he would need a visa to travel to that country.

The man said, "Oh, I don't need that. I've been to China many times for work, and I've never had one of those."

Confused, the clerk double-checked his records and replied, "I'm sorry, sir. Your stay will require a visa."

When he heard this, the man was annoyed. He responded, "Okay, I've been to China multiple times. Every single time, they have accepted my American Express!"

· ▰ ·

Q: How do you know the **moon** is going broke?
A: It's down to its last **quarter**.

Q: What lands as often on its **tail** as it does its **head**?

A: A **penny**.

························· 〰 ·····························

Q: Why was the **coach** yelling at a vending machine?

A: He wanted his **quarter back**.

NATURE'S NONSENSE

Q: What does a cloud do when it gets an **itch**?
A: It finds the nearest sky**scraper**.

* * *

I'm so **bright** that my dad calls me **son**.

* * *

Q: Why don't you wear **snow** boots?
A: Because they will **melt**.

Did you hear about the riots on **Mars**? The government declared **Martian** law.

.... 👄 ....

Q: What does a cow make when the sun comes out?
A: A shadow.

.... 👄 ....

I was trying to catch some **fog** earlier but I **mist**.

.... 👄 ....

Q: Why was the cat afraid of the **tree**?
A: Because of its **bark**.

.... 👄 ....

Did you hear about the restaurant on the **moon**?
Great food, no **atmosphere**.

.... 👄 ....

Q: In which **state** does the Ohio River run?
A: In the **liquid** state.

The only thing that **flat**-earthers fear is **sphere** itself.

· ⌣ ·

Q: What kind of **hair** do oceans have?
A: Wavy.

· ⌣ ·

A Russian couple is walking down a street in Moscow when the husband feels a drop hit his nose.

"I think it's raining," he says to his wife.

"No, that feels like snow to me, dear," she replies.

Just then, a Communist Party official walks toward them. "Let's not fight about it," the man says. "Let's ask Comrade Rudolph whether it's officially raining or snowing."

"It's raining, of course," Comrade Rudolph says and walks on.

But the woman insists, "I know that felt like snow."

To which the man quietly says, "Rudolph the Red knows rain, dear."

· ⌣ ·

I have a hard time trusting **trees**. They seem kind of **shady**.

Q: What **runs** all day but never gets tired?
A: Water.

· ～ ·

Orion's **Belt** is a big **waist** of space.

· ～ ·

Q: What is **sticky** and brown?
A: A **stick**.

· ～ ·

Q: How many apples grow on a tree?
A: All of them.

· ～ ·

Mountains aren't just funny. They're **hill areas**.

· ～ ·

I stayed up all night wondering where the **sun** had gone. Then it **dawned** on me.

Q: How do you find your dog if it's lost in the **woods**?

A: Put your ear up to a tree and listen for the **bark**!

.... ~ ....

Q: What do you use to cut the **ocean**?

A: A **sea**saw.

.... ~ ....

For years, I've suspected my wife of adding soil to my **garden**. When I asked her about it, she just shrugged. The **plot** thickens...

.... ~ ....

Q: What's the **scariest** plant in the forest?

A: Bam**boo**.

.... ~ ....

I'd like to know how the earth **rotates**. It would make my **day**.

Q: What's a **tree's** favorite drink?
A: **Root** beer.

Q: What lies on the **ocean floor**, twitching uncontrollably?
A: A nervous **wreck**.

Did you hear about the **quarry** that went out of business? They hit **rock** bottom.

Q: What did the dad **volcano** say to his son?
A: "I **lava** you."

R.I.P. **boiled water**. You will be **mist**!

Q: What did the ground say to the **earthquake**?
A: "You **crack** me up!"

Plateaus are the **highest** form of **flat**tery.

Q: How can you take a bath **without water**?
A: You **sun**bathe.

Two botanists were working on a research project together. In all seriousness, one turned to the other and said, "You know, this job may not be the most poplar, but I do love it."

The other botanist stared blankly at the first and didn't respond.

The first one continued, "If you're not a fan of tree puns, you can leaf me alone. Maybe they're just oak-ay to some people, but I fernly beleaf my jokes are qualitree."

The other botanist walked away without saying a word.

Q: What planet is like a **circus**?
A: Saturn, because it has **three rings**.

· · · · · · · · · · · · · · · · · · · ~~~ · · · · · · · · · · · · · · · · · · ·

Rivers are so lazy. They never get out of their **beds**.

· · · · · · · · · · · · · · · · · · · ~~~ · · · · · · · · · · · · · · · · · · ·

Q: What happens to nitrogen when the **sun** comes up?
A: It becomes **day**trogen.

· · · · · · · · · · · · · · · · · · · ~~~ · · · · · · · · · · · · · · · · · · ·

Q: How do **trees** access the internet?
A: They **log** on.

PROFESSIONALLY

SPEAKING

Did you hear about the burglar who fell into the **cement** mixer? Now he's a **hardened** criminal.

Q: At what time do most people go to the **dentist**?
A: At **tooth-hurty**.

A firefighter told me my **smoke detectors** were too old, but they work just fine. I think he was being **alarm**ist.

I heard the **steamroller** driver was complimented for doing a good job. He was **flat**tered.

Q: How do **bartenders** surf the web?
A: On the **gin**ternet.

Did you hear about the guy who was fired from the **keyboard** factory? He wasn't putting in enough **shifts**.

Q: Why did the **electrician** close early on Mondays?
A: Because business was very **light**.

I'm not happy being a **glue** salesman, but I **stick** with it!

A man goes to the eye doctor because he is having vision trouble. When he enters, the receptionist asks him why he is there.

The man complains, "Well, I keep seeing spots in front of my eyes."

The receptionist asks, "Have you ever seen a doctor before?"

And the man replies, "No, just spots."

. . . .   ━   . . . .

Q: Why does an **actor** enjoy his work so much?
A: Because it's all **play**.

. . . .   ━   . . . .

I know an **archaeologist** who had to change professions. Her career is in **ruins**!

. . . .   ━   . . . .

Q: When do **astronauts** eat?
A: At **launch** time!

That **cowboy's** a lot of laughs. He's always **horsing** around.

· ～ ·

Q: What do you get if you cross an **Egyptian** mummy with a car **mechanic**?
A: Tut and Car Man.

· ～ ·

A farmer plowed his field with a **steamroller** because he wanted to grow **mashed** potatoes.

· ～ ·

Q: What did the magician say when he made his **rabbit** disappear?
A: Hare today, gone tomorrow.

· ～ ·

Be quiet inside the **pharmacy**. You might wake the **sleeping** pills.

Q: Why did the farmer fence in the **bull**?
A: She had too much of a **steak** in him to let him go!

· ～ ·

I've always admired **fishermen**. Now those are **reel** men.

· ～ ·

Q: What's the worst **drink** for a soccer player?
A: Penal**tea**.

· ～ ·

My **landlord** has been telling me that he feels inadequate lately. I wonder if he has a **complex**.

· ～ ·

Did you hear about the composer who won't get out of **bed**? He writes a lot of **sheet** music.

As a lawyer, the number of **wrongful convictions** shouldn't surprise me. After all, it's just **trial and error**.

························ ·•· ························

I went to a **dentist's** funeral yesterday. I guess he's filled his last **cavity**.

························ ·•· ························

Q: Why would a **golfer** wear two pairs of pants?
A: In case he gets a **hole in one**.

························ ·•· ························

I confronted a **mime** today. He did **unspeakable** things.

························ ·•· ························

Did you hear about the **dancer's** birthday? It was a **tappy** one!

Q: What kind of burger tells your **fortune**?
A: A **medium** burger!

· ~ ·

I just finished my first day of **excavation** training.
So far I'm really **digging** it.

· ~ ·

I used to be a **bartender** for the mob. It was
whiskey business.

· ~ ·

Q: What should a good lawyer wear to **court**?
A: A proper **lawsuit**.

· ~ ·

I went to a **bridge** builders' seminar. It was
absolutely **rivet**ing.

A group of friars were behind on their belfry payments, and in order to raise funds, they decided to open up a small flower shop.

Their shop became wildly popular, as everyone liked helping the friars out, and a rival florist across town thought the competition was unfair. He asked the good fathers to close down, but they would not. The florist returned another time to beg the friars to close, and they ignored him.

As a last resort, the rival florist hired Hugh Martin, the roughest and most vicious thug in town, to "persuade" the friars to close. Hugh injured them and destroyed most of their store, warning that he would come back if they didn't close up shop.

Terrified, the friars closed the store, thereby proving that Hugh, and only Hugh, can prevent florist friars.

. . . . 🖜 . . . .

Did you see that fight between film **actors**? It was **Star** Wars.

. . . . 🖜 . . . .

Q: What did the cook say to the **dough**?
A: "I **knead** you!"

If you ever open your own business, try selling **stoves**. You'll offer a **range** of **hot** products.

························ 🥸 ························

Q: Why do firefighters wear red suspenders?
A: To keep their pants up.

························ 🥸 ························

If I were an **executioner**, I would prefer to use an axe. It's easier to get a**head**.

························ 🥸 ························

I have a joke about **construction**, but I'm still **working** on it.

························ 🥸 ························

Q: What kind of doctor does a duck visit?
A: A **ducktor**.

A **boxer** started dating a pretty girl. I hear she is a **knockout**!

.... 〰 ....

I once worked as an **ice** delivery driver. **Coolest** job I've ever had.

.... 〰 ....

Q: What do you call a **priest** that becomes a **lawyer**?
A: A **father-in-law**.

.... 〰 ....

Track runners are my inspiration. They get over every **hurdle** in their way.

.... 〰 ....

Q: Why did the police officer **cry** over a ticket?
A: It was a **moving** violation.

I think I want to quit my job. I'd rather clean **mirrors** for a living. It's just something I can **see** myself doing.

· ～ ·

I was a **doctor** for a while but then I quit. Not enough **patience**.

· ～ ·

Did you hear about the two **podiatrists** who opened their offices on the same street? They were **arch** enemies.

· ～ ·

Q: Why did the clown wear **loud** socks?
A: So his feet wouldn't **fall asleep**.

· ～ ·

The lady helping me at the **bank** has a big stain on her shirt. Should I **teller**?

Did you hear about the **fortuneteller's** vacation? She went to **Palm** Beach.

.... 〰 ....

Q: Why did the cowboy ride his horse?
A: Because the horse was too heavy to carry.

.... 〰 ....

I asked my doctor if the ointment she prescribed would clear up my **skin** spots, but she said she never makes **rash** promises.

.... 〰 ....

Just because this guy is the only **chimney** sweep in town, he thinks he can raise his prices **through the roof**!

.... 〰 ....

Q: Why did the **janitor** take early retirement?
A: Because he realized that **grime** doesn't pay.

Business is slow these days at the **medicine** factory. You can really hear a **cough drop**.

·························· 👄 ··························

The sexiest people tend to be **runners**. They're quite at**track**tive.

·························· 👄 ··························

Q: How do **ironworkers** order their steaks?
A: Weld done!

·························· 👄 ··························

Did you hear about the **bored** banker? He lost **interest** in everything.

·························· 👄 ··························

Q: What did the **janitor** say when he popped out of the closet?
A: "**Supplies!**"

A doctor made it his regular habit to stop at a bar for a hazelnut daiquiri on his way home from work each night. The bartender knew of his habit and would always have the drink waiting at precisely 5:03 p.m.

One afternoon, as the end of the workday approached, the bartender was dismayed to find that he was out of hazelnut extract. Thinking quickly, he threw together a daiquiri made with hickory nuts and set it on the bar.

The doctor came in at his regular time, took one sip of the drink, and exclaimed, "This isn't a hazelnut daiquiri!"

"No, I'm sorry," replied the bartender. "It's a hickory daiquiri, Doc."

······························· 👨 ·······························

My dad always said, "Don't be quick to find **faults**."
He was a good man, but a terrible **geologist**.

······························· 👨 ·······························

Q: What burgers make great **actors**?
A: Hamburgers.

Yesterday, a **clown** held the door open for me. I thought it was a nice **jester**.

.... ～ ....

I like when people stick their **noses** in my business. My company makes **tissues**.

.... ～ ....

Q: What do you use to steal a photographer's **legs**?
A: A **Knee**kon.

.... ～ ....

My dad used to always say, "The sky's **the limit**!" That's probably why he got fired as an **astronaut** from NASA.

.... ～ ....

I used to work at a **shoe** factory, but my **sole** wasn't in it.

Q: Who is the most **grateful** actor?
A: T. Hanks.

Q: When does a **farmer** dance?
A: When the **beet** drops.

A doctor broke his leg when he was auditioning for a **play**. Luckily, he still made the **cast**.

Don't trust **acupuncturists**. They're **backstabbers**.

STUCK ON STEM

Computer programmers never go outside. There are too many **bugs**.

········· 🥸 ·········

I told my dad a joke about **electricity** once. He said it was so funny it **hertz**.

········· 🥸 ·········

Q: Why did the dog's owner think her dog was a great mathematician?
A: When she asked the dog what **six minus six** was, the dog said **nothing**.

I'm reading a book about **antigravity**. It's impossible to put **down**.

.... 👨 ....

Q: How does **NASA** organize a party?
A: They **planet**.

.... 👨 ....

Scientists have discovered a giant, naturally occurring **windmill**. They say it's Mother Nature's biggest **fan**.

.... 👨 ....

Q: What did the dentist say to the **computer**?
A: "This won't hurt a **byte**."

.... 👨 ....

I thought I would tell you a good **time-travel** joke, but you **didn't** like it.

Q: What did one **math** book say to the other?

A: "Man, I've got a lot of **problems**!"

⋯⋯⋯⋯⋯⋯⋯⋯ 〰 ⋯⋯⋯⋯⋯⋯⋯⋯

Einstein finally developed a theory about **space**. It was about **time** too!

⋯⋯⋯⋯⋯⋯⋯⋯ 〰 ⋯⋯⋯⋯⋯⋯⋯⋯

During wartime, a chemistry teacher was recruited by the military as a radio operator. Soon he became familiar with the military's habit of abbreviating everything. One day, as his unit came under sustained attack, he was asked to urgently inform his HQ what was happening.

He shouted the report over the radio, "NaCl over NaOH! NaCl over NaOH!"

"NaCl over NaOH?" asked his officer. "What do you mean by that?"

The chemist responded, "The base is under a salt!"

⋯⋯⋯⋯⋯⋯⋯⋯ 〰 ⋯⋯⋯⋯⋯⋯⋯⋯

"Dad, my tablet's battery is **dead**."

"Well, we better go **bury** it then."

Q: What is a computer's favorite **food**?
A: Micro**chips**.

· ~ ·

To the guy who invented **zero**: thanks for **nothing**.

· ~ ·

Q: What do they teach in **hamburger** math courses?
A: The **meat**ric system!

· ~ ·

Did you hear that joke about **robots**? It really grinds my **gears**.

· ~ ·

Two **satellites** got married on Saturday. The **reception** was fantastic.

Q: What does a baby computer call its **father**?
A: Data.

.... 〰 ....

Atoms are untrustworthy little things. They **make up** everything.

.... 〰 ....

Q: Why did the **physics** teacher break up with the **biology** teacher?
A: Because there was no **chemistry**.

.... 〰 ....

I got a universal **remote** for Christmas. This **changes** everything!

.... 〰 ....

Q: What do you call a tube with a **degree**?
A: A **graduated** cylinder.

There's something about **subtraction** that just doesn't **add** up.

.... 👨 ....

Q: What's the longest piece of furniture in a school?
A: The **multiplication** table.

.... 👨 ....

I never understood **odor**less chemicals. They never make **scents**.

.... 👨 ....

My favorite frequency is 50,000 **Hz**. You've probably never **heard** it before.

.... 👨 ....

Q: Where does bad **light** end up?
A: In **prism**.

Never discuss **infinity** with a mathematician. They can go on about it **forever**.

Myfriend asked to hear a **potassium** joke. I said, "**K**."

Q: Why are **chemists** great for solving problems?
A: They have all the **solutions**.

Organic **chemistry** is difficult. Those who study it have **alkynes** of trouble.

My friend bought me a **telekinetic abacus** for my birthday. It wasn't my favorite present, but it's the **thought** that **counts**.

"Dad, do you know any jokes about **sodium**?"

"**Na**."

················· 〰 ·················

I had to make all these bad **chemistry** jokes because all the good ones **Argon**.

················· 〰 ·················

Never trust someone with **graph** paper. They're always **plotting** something.

················· 〰 ·················

Q: Do robots have sisters?
A: No, just tran**sistors**!

················· 〰 ·················

Nitrous oxide is no **laughing** matter. Oh wait, yes it is!

Q: What process is a **house** in if it is trying to be the same inside?
A: Homeostasis.

· 〰 ·

When I leave a sandwich on my **computer** desk, I always discover a couple of **megabytes** taken out of it.

· 〰 ·

Q: What technology gets the **Starship *Enterprise*** moving?
A: Spock plugs.

· 〰 ·

My friend genetically modifies **salad**. She is a **rocket** scientist.

Q: Do you know what the worst part about **PC RAM** is?

A: No matter how much light you shine, it's still **SO-DIMM**.

· ·　～　· ·

I can't use my **laptop** anymore because someone spilled apple juice on it. It was a **cider** attack.

· ·　～　· ·

Two atoms were walking in opposite directions when they accidentally ran into each other.

After picking itself up off the ground, one atom said to the other, "Oh, I'm so sorry! Are you all right?"

The other atom replied, "No, I lost an electron."

"Are you absolutely sure?" asked the first atom.

"Yeah, I'm positive."

· ·　～　· ·

I hate **negative numbers** and I will **stop at nothing** to avoid them.

Q: What do you do with a **dead** chemist?
A: You **barium**.

·····

I left my **PC** on all night, and when I woke up, it was **freezing**. Turns out, I left the **Windows** open.

·····

Q: What is **email's** least favorite food?
A: Spam.

·····

I would tell you a **chemistry** joke, but I doubt it would get a **reaction**.

·····

Q: Have you heard of the band 999**MB**?
A: They haven't got a **gig** yet.

·····

I changed my iPod™ name to **Titanic**. It is **syncing** now.

TRAFFIC STOPS BUT THE DAD JOKES WON'T

I had a dream that I was a **muffler** last night. I woke up **exhaust**ed!

* * *

Q: Why do chicken coops only have **two doors**?
A: Because if they had four, they would be chicken **sedans**!

* * *

Q: What did the first **stoplight** say to the second stoplight?
A: "Don't look! I'm **changing**!"

A man gets into a parked taxicab. He taps the driver on the shoulder to tell the driver the address he's going to. The driver screams.

After composing himself, the driver says, "Don't *ever* do that again. You scared the daylights out of me!"

The passenger apologizes, "I'm so sorry! But didn't you know I was going to get in and tell you where to go?"

The driver replies, "It's not your fault. Today is my first day as a cab driver. I've been driving a hearse for the last twenty-five years!"

Q: What **driver** doesn't have a license?
A: A **screwdriver**.

If **goods** are damaged in transport, do they become **bads**?

Q: What part of a car is the **laziest**?
A: The wheels. They are always **tired**.

Q: What happens when a **frog's** car breaks down?
A: It gets **toad** away.

.... 👨 ....

Q: What do you get if you cross a bike and a **rose**?
A: Bicycle **petals**!

.... 👨 ....

I've spent twenty years performing maintenance on **limos** but I've got nothing to **chauffeur** it.

.... 👨 ....

Q: How do you stop a dog from barking in the **back** of a car?
A: Put him in the **front**.

.... 👨 ....

Q: Why didn't the dinosaur cross the road?
A: Because roads weren't invented yet.

Did you hear about the **truck** driver who got a flat **tire**? It was a **wheelie** bad time.

.... 👨 ....

Q: What has a horn and gives milk?
A: A milk truck.

.... 👨 ....

Q: What do you call a man with a **car** on his head?
A: Jack!

.... 👨 ....

Q: When does a car stop being a car?
A: When it turns into a driveway.

.... 👨 ....

I can't get my **bicycle** to stand up by itself. I think it's because it's two-**tired**.

Q: What kind of a car does a **crazy** man drive?
A: A **loco**motive.

························· 〰 ·························

Q: What did the bus conductor say to the **frog**?
A: "**Hop** on."

························· 〰 ·························

My new job involves working with **aircrafts**, but it's a bit **plane**.

························· 〰 ·························

Q: What kind of car drives **over water**?
A: Any kind of car if it's on a **bridge**.

························· 〰 ·························

Q: Where do cars get the most **flat tires**?
A: Where there is a **fork** in the road.

Q: Which kind of **snakes** are found on cars?
A: Windshield **vipers**.

.... 〰 ....

Q: What kind of **ears** do trains have?
A: **Engineers**.

.... 〰 ....

Did you hear about the boy who had to do a project about **trains**? He had to keep **track** of everything!

.... 〰 ....

Q: What did the bicycle call its **dad**?
A: **Pop**cycle.

.... 〰 ....

Q: Why was the man driving in his **swimsuit**?
A: He was in a car**pool**.

The woman who was hit by a **car** felt very **tire**d the next day.

························· ✦ ·························

Q: Why did the **bat** miss the bus?
A: Because he **hung** around for too long.

························· ✦ ·························

An officer pulled me over for driving in **circles**. I was just going for a little **spin**!

························· ✦ ·························

Q: Why do **barbers** make good drivers?
A: Because they know all the short **cuts**.

························· ✦ ·························

Q: Why did the man put his car in the **oven**?
A: Because he wanted a **hot** rod.

A famous art thief attempted to steal paintings from the Louvre in Paris, but he was caught only two blocks away from the scene of the crime because his van ran out of gas.

When the police found him on the side of the road, all the thief could say for himself was, "I had no Monet to buy Degas to make the van Gogh. But I had to try stealing the paintings and making my getaway because I had nothing Toulouse!"

* * *

Q: How do eels get around the seabed?
A: By **octobus**.

* * *

Garbage collectors are **rubbish** drivers.

* * *

Q: Why did the **noodle** get a driving ticket?
A: It drove **pasta** stop sign.

Q: How do you take a **pig** to the hospital?
A: By **ham**bulance!

Q: How do **bees** get to school?
A: By school **buzz**!

Q: How do you get **Pikachu**™ on a bus?
A: You **poke-'em-on**!

I owe a lot to **sidewalks**. They've been keeping me off the **streets** for years.

Q: Why did no one take the bus to school?
A: It wouldn't fit through the door.

Q: What's the **hardest** thing about learning to ride a bicycle?
A: The **road**.

⚬⚬⚬⚬⚬⚬⚬⚬⚬⚬⚬⚬⚬⚬⚬⚬⚬⚬⚬⚬⚬⚬⚬⚬⚬⚬⚬⚬⚬⚬⚬⚬⚬⚬⚬⚬⚬⚬⚬

I have a friend who is obsessed with monorails. All she ever talks about these days is monorails—how fast they go, how great they look, how amazing it is that they speed along on just one, single rail. She really has a one-track mind.

⚬⚬⚬⚬⚬⚬⚬⚬⚬⚬⚬⚬⚬⚬⚬⚬⚬⚬⚬⚬⚬⚬⚬⚬⚬⚬⚬⚬⚬⚬⚬⚬⚬⚬⚬⚬⚬⚬⚬

Q: What do you call a **settee** with an outboard motor?
A: A high-speed **chaise**.

⚬⚬⚬⚬⚬⚬⚬⚬⚬⚬⚬⚬⚬⚬⚬⚬⚬⚬⚬⚬⚬⚬⚬⚬⚬⚬⚬⚬⚬⚬⚬⚬⚬⚬⚬⚬⚬⚬⚬

I'm not addicted to **brake** fluid. I can **stop** whenever I want.

⚬⚬⚬⚬⚬⚬⚬⚬⚬⚬⚬⚬⚬⚬⚬⚬⚬⚬⚬⚬⚬⚬⚬⚬⚬⚬⚬⚬⚬⚬⚬⚬⚬⚬⚬⚬⚬⚬⚬

Q: What do you call a laughing **motorcycle**?
A: **Yamaha**haha.

Q: What kind of car does a **sheep** drive?
A: Su**baa**ru.

.... 〜 ....

Did you hear about the crime in the **parking garage**? It was wrong on so many **levels**.

.... 〜 ....

I couldn't figure out how to fasten my **seatbelt**. Then it **clicked**.

.... 〜 ....

Q: What do you call a **depressed** traffic jam?
A: **Bummer**-to-**bummer** traffic.

WORLD'S
BEST
DAD
(JOKES)